OWN IT! EMBRACE YOUR

Faith Journal

by ChellBee

ISBN-13: 978-1544170084
ISBN-10: 1544170084

CONTENTS

WELCOME FROM CHELLBEE

I'm so glad you've decided to become intentional about your relationship with God. Embracing your spiritual journey is not always the easiest decision to make. After all, no one ever really knows where to start. We go to church, try to read the bible, buy books, and check out blogs. Typically along the way, we lose focus, motivation, or the ability to develop a routine that enables us to fully strengthen our relationship with God the way we envisioned.

Believe me, I have been there time and time again. I finally found a method that worked. I was able to gain a better understanding of the word, accomplish a long term reading goal, and be consistent. But I still felt there was something missing and I knew that most of us don't have the time to research, create, recreate, and rethink how to get started.

Beginning to be intentional about your spiritual journey is an easy decision to make but difficult to stay consistent with. It was important to me that you have the tools you need to not only get started but stay consistent in your spiritual journey. All you need to get started is a bible and this book.

Whether you're just getting started or ready to take your spiritual journey to another level. I'm so excited you took the first step. Just remember it's not enough to get started, you have to stick with it, and be consistent. Consistency is the key to change. So let's rock it out together.

Before you get started read the how to section which highlight tips for using the journal. I have included my personal journal as a sample in case you need further direction. If you don't know where to start reading there are 3 different reading plan. You will find the reading plans are book by book and not piecemeal. The best way to better understand the Bible is to read each book in its entirety.

These methods have transformed my spiritual journey. Embracing my faith is the best thing that ever happened to me. I have been moved to do things I never imagined, including this book. It's amazing how your life can be transformed by releasing control and trusting God.

With Love,

ChellBee

CHRIST SCRIPTURE READING PLAN

WEEK 1

Day 1 Matthew 1

Day 2 Matthew 2

Day 3 Matthew 3

Day 4 Matthew 4

Day 5 Matthew 5

Day 6 Matthew 6

Day 7 Matthew 7

WEEK 2

Day 8 Matthew 8

Day 9 Matthew 9

Day 10 Matthew 10

Day 11 Matthew 11

Day 12 Matthew 12

Day 13 Matthew 13:1-30

Day 14 Jeremiah 13:31-35

WEEK 3

Day 15 Matthew 14

Day 16 Matthew 15

Day 17 Matthew 16

Day 18 Matthew 17

Day 19 Matthew 18

Day 20 Matthew 19

Day 21 Matthew 20

WEEK 4

Day 22 Matthew 21

Day 23 Matthew 22

Day 24 Matthew 23

Day 25 Matthew 24

Day 26 Matthew 25

Day 27 Matthew 26

Day 28 Matthew 27

Whoever does not take up their cross and *follow* me is not
worthy of me.
Matthew 10:38

CHRIST SCRIPTURE READING PLAN

WEEK 5

Day 29 Matthew 28

Day 30 John 1

Day 31 John 2

Day 32 John 3

Day 33 John 4

Day 34 John 5

Day 35 John 6:1-21

WEEK 6

Day 36 John 6:22-71

Day 37 John 7

Day 38 John 8

Day 39 John 9

Day 30 John 10

Day 41 John 11

Day 42 John 12

WEEK 7

Day 43 John 13

Day 44 John 14

Day 45 John 15

Day 46 John 16

Day 47 John 17

Day 48 John 18

Day 49 John 19

WEEK 8

Day 50 John 20

Day 51 John 21

Day 52 Colossians 1

Day 53 Colossians 2

Day 54 Colossians 3

Day 55 Colossians 4

Jesus said, "Did I not tell you that if you *believe*, you will see the glory of God?"
John 11:40

HOPE SCRIPTURE READING PLAN

WEEK 1

Day 1 Jeremiah 1

Day 2 Jeremiah 2

Day 3 Jeremiah 3

Day 4 Jeremiah 4

Day 5 Jeremiah 5-6

Day 6 Jeremiah 7

Day 7 Jeremiah 8

WEEK 2

Day 8 Jeremiah 9

Day 9 Jeremiah 10

Day 10 Jeremiah 11

Day 11 Jeremiah 12

Day 12 Jeremiah 13-14

Day 13 Jeremiah 15

Day 14 Jeremiah 16

WEEK 3

Day 15 Jeremiah 18

Day 16 Jeremiah 19

Day 17 Jeremiah 20

Day 18 Jeremiah 21

Day 19 Jeremiah 22

Day 20 Jeremiah 23

Day 21 Jeremiah 24

WEEK 4

Day 22 Jeremiah 25

Day 23 Jeremiah 26

Day 24 Jeremiah 27

Day 25 Jeremiah 28

Day 26 Jeremiah 29

Day 27 Jeremiah 30

Day 28 Jeremiah 31

Be joyful in *hope*, patient in affliction, faithful in prayer.

Romans 12:12

HOPE SCRIPTURE READING PLAN

WEEK 5

Day 29 Jeremiah 32

Day 30 Jeremiah 33

Day 31 Jeremiah 34

Day 32 Jeremiah 35

Day 33 Jeremiah 36

Day 34 Jeremiah 37

Day 35 Jeremiah 38

WEEK 6

Day 36 Jeremiah 39

Day 37 Jeremiah 40

Day 38 Jeremiah 41

Day 39 Jeremiah 42

Day 30 Jeremiah 43

Day 41 Jeremiah 44

Day 42 Jeremiah 45

WEEK 7

Day 43 Jeremiah 46

Day 44 Jeremiah 47

Day 45 Jeremiah 48

Day 46 Jeremiah 49

Day 47 Jeremiah 50

Day 48 Jeremiah 51

Day 49 Jeremiah 52

WEEK 8

Day 50 1 Peters 1

Day 51 1 Peters 2

Day 52 1 Peters 3

Day 53 1 Peters 4

Day 54 1 Peters 5

But blessed is the one who trusts in the Lord, whose confidence is in him.
Jeremiah 17:7

LOVE SCRIPTURE READING PLAN

WEEK 1

Day 1 Song of Solomon 1:1-7

Day 2 Song of Solomon 1:8-17

Day 3 Song of Solomon 2:1-7

Day 4 Song of Solomon 2:8-17

Day 5 Song of Solomon 3:1-5

Day 6 Song of Solomon 3:6-11

Day 7 Song of Solomon 4

WEEK 2

Day 8 Song of Solomon 5:1-9

Day 9 Song of Solomon 5:10-16

Day 10 Song of Solomon 6

Day 11 Song of Solomon 7

Day 12 Song of Solomon 8:1-7

Day 13 Song of Solomon 8:8-14

Day 14 1 John 1

WEEK 3

Day 15 1 John 2:1-14

Day 16 1 John 2:15-26

Day 17 1 John 3

Day 18 1 John 4:1-7

Day 19 1 John 4:7-21

Day 20 1 John 5

Day 21 2 John

Anyone who does not *love* does not know God, because God is

love.

1 John 4:8

HOW TO USE YOUR FAITH JOURNAL

There are many approaches to studying the bible from Bible art, group Bible studies, to independent reading. Your experience with the Bible is whatever you make of it. The most important thing about studying the bible is getting started and sticking with it. Praise and worship are great but creating a one on one relationship with God is amazing. By committing to reading the Bible daily you gain a deeper understanding and connection to the word.

Bible Journal

The method I use to study the Bible also helps to create a consistent prayer life. Keep it simple! No matter where you are on your spiritual journey you don't need much for these techniques to work. The type of Bible you use is completely up to you. Make sure you choose a version that is easy to read. If you don't already own a Bible make sure to skim over it before purchasing to ensure it is a good fit. A study bible is a great option if you want access to reference notes to gain a better understanding. No half stepping!

Make the commitment to yourself that bible journaling will be a part of your daily routine. Plan for at least 15-30 minutes of quiet time. Start journaling every day first thing in the morning. Grab a cup of coffee, tea, or cocoa and get cozy with your bible and journal. You can read as many or as few verses as you would like. I don't recommend reading more than 2 chapters per a sitting. There are no rules! So make it your own.

Ultimately this technique is the simplest way I have found to study the Bible. The purpose of bible journaling or studying the bible is not to be an expert. But to try to gain a better understanding of the word for yourself.

Consequently, *faith* comes from hearing the message, and the message is heard through the word about Christ.
Romans 10:17

Reading the Bible is an opportunity to learn something new about the world, yourself, and life lessons. There will be times where you read the same book or chapters multiple times to gain a better understanding. You must commit to creating, maintaining, and developing a one on one relationship with God.

Bible Mapping

Bible mapping will also help you easily identify questions you had. There will be times when you will be unsure about what you read or how it applies to your life. Bible journaling is the opportunity to think through those questions. Ultimately, this journal will serve as a reference for you and the changes God has made possible in your life.

There will be times during your studies when you will encounter unfamiliar terms. But using this method ensures you can easily study the bible and reference your notes. If you are for any reason unable to come to an understanding, be sure to use your resources at church. Speak with your pastoral staff about any questions you have. If you don't yet have a church home, many spirituals leaders are on social media and would love to engage with you about the word. Whatever you do don't allow your questions to go unanswered.

Circle Words to define.

Highlight phrases that stand out.

Wavy Line Words and events you want to know more about.

Box Words and phrases you want to Memorize.

The Holy Spirit, whom the Father will send in my name, will teach you all things and will remind you of everything I have said to you.

John 14:26

Bible Journaling Method

I Heard You Read however many scriptures you would like. Write down the verse (s) that speak to you.

I Thank You For What revelation did you have that made you thankful.

I Observed Summarize your observations about what you read. What were the major occurrences, what stood out, and what was the sentiments.

I Learned What lessons did you learn and how did it make you feel? How does what you read apply to your life?

I Pray Based on what you read, what do you want to tell God. What do you need his help with.

Faith Journal

There will be moments when you feel as though you can hear God talking to you. You'll have thoughts and answers to problems that you know you didn't think of. You'll begin to do things and see a future for yourself you never thought you were capable of.

If we confess our sins, he is _faithful_ and just.
1 John 1:9

You may be praying to God just hoping to be able to afford to pay your bills. Even though the word says he wants you to be prosperous. Don't allow self-doubt, fear, and your current circumstances to make you believe that God doesn't want you to be prosperous.

Remember your spiritual journey is about you. Be responsible. You need to give up the blame mindset if you want to reach the heights God has for you. There will always be things that cause you soul wounds. You must choose either to be a victim or victor, but you can't be both. Recommit to God. Our life is about how we can glorify God's Kingdom and empower others to do the same.

Walk in *obedience* and keep his commands.

1 Kings 2:3

Dreams Write down how you are going to use your skills to glorify God's Kingdom.

Verses to Live by Write down verses that remind you of the life and kind of person God wants you to be.

Confessions Write down your thoughts, past, and actions that are stopping you from living according to the word.

God, I need your help to write down the what is holding you back from God's glory. Because giving up is not an option.

Prayer Journal

Originally, I underestimated the strength of writing down my prayers. I came to realize writing down my prayers empowered me and boosted my confidence. Creating a prayer life strengthens your faith and connection to God.

Use your time of prayer as an opportunity to give thanks. I know it's tempting but don't spend your prayer time going over your wish list. Remember God knows your every need, pending trials, tribulation, and triumphs. In those times of needs where you do bring your problems to God, trust him to change it, and have faith that he will do so when he feels it's time. To be your best in your spiritual journey you must pray consistently and possess unwavering child-like faith in God's abilities.

Have a prayer attitude of _gratitude_ and not petition!

Those in need of Prayer Write down any prayer request you received or anyone you want to pray for.

Lord we Praise your name thank God for your blessings.

Thank You for Answering my Prayers acknowledge God for the prayers he's already answered.

REST method for becoming Consistent

Routine Make journaling a part of your daily routine. Consistency is the key so decide on a time and stick to it. Studies show it takes at least 21 days to form a habit. The key to consistency is creating a good habit. If your morning hygiene is your only routine then journal after.

Engage Great way to form new habits is by participate in a Christian community or seeking an accountability partner. We are always more likely to succeed when surrounded with a strong group of like minded individuals.

Silence Choose a quiet place to journal. Be prepared for journaling before hand. Every minute counts so remove any distractions including your cell phones. So that you can really focus and mediate on the word.

Temperament Most importantly have a positive attitude. Get excited about journaling and spending this time with God and his word. Your attitude will be the determining factor in your journaling.

You don't have to beg and plead with God, so just pray.

This Journal

belongs

to

_____

With unbreakable *faith*, understated abilities, and unmatched work *ethic*. You can achieve your *dreams*!

WEEK *One*

I *will*

I'm *thankful* for _____

_____

_____

_____

_____

_____

Verse to *live* by

And if we know that he *hears* us—whatever we ask—we know
that we have what we asked of him.
1 John 5:15

Those in need of *prayer*

Thank you for answering my prayers _____

_____
_____
_____
_____
_____
_____
_____
_____
_____
_____

Lord we *Praise* your name

Bible Journal

I Thank You for

I Heard You

I Observed

I Learned

I Pray

Bible Journal

I Thank You for

I Heard You _____

_____
_____
_____
_____

I Observed

I Learned _____

_____
_____
_____
_____
_____
_____

I Pray

Bible Journal

VERSES READ   DATE

I Thank You for

I Heard You

I Observed

I Learned

I Pray

Faith Journal

Dreams

Confessions

_____

_____
_____
_____
_____
_____
_____
_____
_____
_____
_____
_____

God *help* me

Bible Journal

I *Thank* You for

I *Heard* You _____

_____

_____

_____

_____

I *Observed*

I *Learned* _____

_____

_____

_____

_____

_____

_____

I *Pray*

Bible Journal

I Thank You for

I Heard You

_____

_____

_____

_____

_____

I Observed

I Learned

_____

_____

_____

_____

_____

_____

_____

I Pray

Bible Journal

VERSES READ   DATE

I *Thank* You for

I *Heard* You _____

_____

_____

_____

_____

I *Observed*

I *Learned* _____

_____

_____

_____

_____

_____

I *Pray*

Bible Journal

_____
VERSES READ

_____
DATE

I *Thank* You for

I *Heard* You _____

_____

_____

_____

_____

I *Observed*

I *Learned* _____

_____

_____

_____

_____

_____

_____

I *Pray*

Prayer Journal   Devote yourselves to prayer, being watchful and thankful.
Colossians 4:2

Those in need of prayer

Thank you for answering my prayers _____

_____

_____

_____

_____

_____

_____

_____

_____

_____

_____

Lord we Praise your name

God gave us a spirit not of fear but of *power* and love and self-control.
2 Timothy 1:7

WEEK *Two*

I *will*

I'm *thankful* for _____

_____

_____

_____

_____

_____

Verse to *live* by

Look to the LORD and his strength; seek his face always.
1 Chronicles 16:11

Those in need of prayer

Thank you for answering my prayers _____

_____

_____

_____

_____

_____

_____

_____

_____

_____

_____

Lord we Praise your name

Bible Journal

I *Thank* You for

I *Heard* You _____

_____
_____
_____
_____

I *Observed*

I *Learned* _____

_____
_____
_____
_____
_____
_____

I *Pray*

Bible Journal

_____   _____
VERSES READ   DATE

I Thank You for

I Heard You _____

_____
_____
_____
_____

I Observed

I Learned _____

_____
_____
_____
_____
_____
_____

I Pray

Bible Journal

I *Thank* You for

I *Heard* You _____

_____

_____

_____

_____

I *Observed*

I *Learned* _____

_____

_____

_____

_____

_____

I *Pray*

Lord, do not hold this *sin* against them.
Acts 7:60

Dreams

Confessions

_____

_____
_____
_____
_____
_____
_____
_____
_____
_____
_____
_____

God *help* me

Bible Journal

I *Thank* You for

I *Heard* You _____

_____

_____

_____

_____

I *Observed*

I *Learned* _____

_____

_____

_____

_____

_____

I *Pray*

Bible Journal

I Thank You for

I Heard You _____

_____

_____

_____

_____

I Observed

I Learned _____

_____

_____

_____

_____

_____

_____

I Pray

Bible Journal

I *Thank* You for

I *Heard* You _____

_____

_____

_____

_____

I *Observed*

I *Learned* _____

_____

_____

_____

_____

_____

I *Pray*

Bible Journal

_____

VERSES READ   DATE

I *Thank* You for

I *Heard* You _____

_____
_____
_____
_____

I *Observed*

I *Learned* _____

_____
_____
_____
_____
_____
_____

I *Pray*

Prayer Journal   You will pray to him, and he will hear you, and you will fulfill
your vows.
Job 22:27

Those in need of prayer

Thank you for answering my prayers _____

_____

_____

_____

_____

_____

_____

_____

_____

_____

Lord we Praise your name

Let not your *hearts* be troubled, neither let them be
afraid.
John 14:27

WEEK *Three*

I *will*

I'm *thankful* for _____

_____

_____

_____

_____

_____

_____

Verse to *live* by

You will seek me and find me, when you seek me with all your heart.
Jeremiah 29:13

Those in need of prayer

Thank you for answering my prayers _____

_____

_____

_____

_____

_____

_____

_____

_____

_____

_____

Lord we Praise your name

Bible Journal

I *Thank* You for

I *Heard* You _____

_____

_____

_____

_____

I *Observed*

I *Learned* _____

_____

_____

_____

_____

_____

I *Pray*

Bible Journal

VERSES READ   DATE

I *Thank* You for

I *Heard* You _____

_____

_____

_____

_____

I *Observed*

I *Learned* _____

_____

_____

_____

_____

_____

_____

I *Pray*

Bible Journal

I *Thank* You for

I *Heard* You _____

_____

_____

_____

_____

I *Observed*

I *Learned* _____

_____

_____

_____

_____

_____

I *Pray*

Faith Journal

Dreams

Confessions

_____

_____

_____

_____

_____

_____

_____

_____

_____

_____

_____

God help me

Bible Journal

I *Thank* You for

I *Heard* You

_____
_____
_____
_____
_____

I *Observed*

I *Learned*

_____
_____
_____
_____
_____
_____

I *Pray*

Bible Journal

VERSES READ   DATE

I Thank You for

I Heard You

I Observed

I Learned

I Pray

Bible Journal

I *Thank* You for

I *Heard* You _____

_____

_____

_____

_____

I *Observed*

I *Learned* _____

_____

_____

_____

_____

_____

I *Pray*

Bible Journal

VERSES READ	DATE

I Thank You for

I Heard You

I Observed

I Learned

I Pray

Prayer Journal   You will pray to him, and he will hear you, and you will fulfill
your vows.
Job 22:27

Those in need of prayer

Thank you for answering my prayers _____

_____
_____
_____
_____
_____
_____
_____
_____
_____
_____

Lord we Praise your name

Let not your *hearts* be troubled, neither let them be afraid.
John 14:27

WEEK *Three*

I *will*

I'm *thankful* for _____
_____
_____
_____
_____
_____
_____

Verse to *live* by

You will seek me and find me, when you seek me with all your heart.
Jeremiah 29:13

Those in need of prayer

Thank you for answering my prayers

_____

_____

_____

_____

_____

_____

_____

_____

_____

_____

Lord we Praise your name

Bible Journal

I *Thank* You for

I *Heard* You

I *Observed*

I *Learned*

I *Pray*

Bible Journal

I *Thank* You for

I *Heard* You _____

_____

_____

_____

_____

I *Observed*

I *Learned* _____

_____

_____

_____

_____

_____

I *Pray*

Bible Journal

I *Thank* You for

I *Heard* You _____

_____

_____

_____

_____

I *Observed*

I *Learned* _____

_____

_____

_____

_____

_____

_____

I *Pray*

Lord, do not hold this sin against them.
Acts 7:60

Dreams

Confessions _____

_____
_____
_____
_____
_____
_____
_____
_____
_____
_____
_____

God help me

Bible Journal

I *Thank* You for

I *Heard* You _____

_____

_____

_____

_____

I *Observed*

I *Learned* _____

_____

_____

_____

_____

_____

_____

I *Pray*

Bible Journal

I Thank You for

I Heard You _____

_____
_____
_____
_____

I Observed

I Learned _____

_____
_____
_____
_____
_____
_____

I Pray

Bible Journal

I Thank You for

I Heard You

I Observed

I Learned

I Pray

Bible Journal

_____   _____
VERSES READ   DATE

I Thank You for

I Heard You _____

_____
_____
_____
_____

I Observed

I Learned _____

_____
_____
_____
_____
_____

I Pray

You will pray to him, and he will hear you, and you will fulfill
your vows.
Job 22:27

Those in need of prayer

Thank you for answering my prayers _____

_____

_____

_____

_____

_____

_____

_____

_____

_____

_____

Lord we Praise your name

Let not your *hearts* be troubled, neither let them be afraid.
John 14:27

WEEK *Four*

I *will*

I'm *thankful* for _____

_____

_____

_____

_____

_____

_____

Verse to *live* by

But I tell you, love your enemies and pray for those who persecute you.
Matthew 5:44

Those in need of prayer

Thank you for answering my prayers _____

_____
_____
_____
_____
_____
_____
_____
_____
_____
_____

Lord we Praise your name

Bible Journal

I Thank You for

I Heard You

I Observed

I Learned

I Pray

Bible Journal

VERSES READ

DATE

I Thank You for

I Heard You _____

_____

_____

_____

_____

I Observed

I Learned _____

_____

_____

_____

_____

_____

I Pray

Bible Journal

I Thank You for

I Heard You

I Observed

I Learned

I Pray

For we live by *faith*, not by sight.
2 Corinthians 5:7

Dreams

Confessions

_____
_____
_____
_____
_____
_____
_____
_____
_____
_____
_____
_____
_____

God *help* me

Bible Journal

_____   _____
VERSES READ   DATE

I Thank You for

I Heard You _____
_____
_____
_____
_____

I Observed

I Learned _____
_____
_____
_____
_____
_____
_____

I Pray

Bible Journal

I Thank You for

I Heard You

I Observed

I Learned

I Pray

Bible Journal

I Thank You for

I Heard You

I Observed

I Learned

I Pray

Bible Journal

I Thank You for

I Heard You

I Observed

I Learned

I Pray

He will respond to the prayer of the destitute; he will not despise their plea.

Psalm 102:17

Those in need of prayer

Thank you for answering my prayers _____

_____

_____

_____

_____

_____

_____

_____

_____

_____

_____

Lord we Praise your name

Trust in the Lord with all your *heart*, and do not
lean on your own understanding.
Proverbs 3:5-6

WEEK *Five*

I *will*

I'm *thankful* for _____

_____

_____

_____

_____

_____

_____

Verse to *live* by

I call on you, my God, for you will answer me; turn your ear to me and hear my prayer.

Psalm 17:6

Those in need of prayer

Thank you for answering my prayers _____

_____

_____

_____

_____

_____

_____

_____

_____

_____

_____

Lord we Praise your name

Bible Journal

I Thank You for

I Heard You

I Observed

I Learned

I Pray

Bible Journal

I *Thank* You for

I *Heard* You _____

_____

_____

_____

_____

I *Observed*

I *Learned* _____

_____

_____

_____

_____

_____

I *Pray*

Bible Journal

VERSES READ   DATE

I Thank You for

I Heard You _____

_____

_____

_____

_____

I Observed

I Learned _____

_____

_____

_____

_____

_____

_____

I Pray

Lord, if You are willing, You can make me *clean*.

Matthew 8:2

Dreams

Confessions

_____

_____

_____

_____

_____

_____

_____

_____

_____

_____

_____

_____

God *help* me

Bible Journal

_____   _____
VERSES READ   DATE

I *Thank* You for

I *Heard* You _____

_____
_____
_____
_____

I *Observed*

I *Learned* _____

_____
_____
_____
_____
_____

I *Pray*

Bible Journal

VERSES READ _____   DATE _____

I Thank You for

I Heard You _____

_____

_____

_____

_____

I Observed

I Learned _____

_____

_____

_____

_____

_____

_____

I Pray

Bible Journal

I Thank You for

I Heard You _____

_____

_____

_____

_____

I Observed

I Learned _____

_____

_____

_____

_____

_____

I Pray

Bible Journal

_____   _____
VERSES READ   DATE

I Thank You for

I Heard You _____
_____
_____
_____
_____

I Observed

I Learned _____
_____
_____
_____
_____
_____
_____

I Pray

Be joyful in hope, patient in affliction, faithful in *prayer*.

Romans 12:12

Those in need of *prayer*

Thank you for answering my prayers _____

_____

_____

_____

_____

_____

_____

_____

_____

_____

_____

Lord we *Praise* your name

Be strong, and let your heart take *courage*, all you
who wait for the Lord!
Psalm 31:24

WEEK Six

I will

I'm thankful for _____

_____
_____
_____
_____
_____
_____

Verse to live by

And if we know that he *hears* us—whatever we ask—we know
that we have what we asked of him.
1 John 5:15

Those in need of *prayer*

Thank you for answering my prayers _____

_____

_____

_____

_____

_____

_____

_____

_____

_____

Lord we *Praise* your name

Bible Journal

I Thank You for

I Heard You

_____

_____

_____

_____

_____

I Observed

I Learned

_____

_____

_____

_____

_____

_____

I Pray

Bible Journal

I *Thank* You for

I *Heard* You _____

_____

_____

_____

_____

I *Observed*

I *Learned* _____

_____

_____

_____

_____

_____

I *Pray*

Bible Journal

VERSES READ   DATE

I Thank You for

I Heard You

_____

_____

_____

_____

_____

I Observed

I Learned

_____

_____

_____

_____

_____

_____

I Pray

Faith Journal

Dreams

Confessions

_____

_____
_____
_____
_____
_____
_____
_____
_____
_____
_____

God *help* me

Bible Journal

DATE

I *Thank* You for

I *Heard* You _____
_____
_____
_____
_____

I *Observed*

I *Learned* _____
_____
_____
_____
_____
_____

I *Pray*

Bible Journal

I Thank You for

I Heard You

I Observed

I Learned

I Pray

Bible Journal

I *Thank* You for

I *Heard* You _____
_____
_____
_____
_____

I *Observed*

I *Learned* _____
_____
_____
_____
_____
_____
_____

I *Pray*

Bible Journal

_____   _____

I *Thank* You for

I *Heard* You _____

_____

_____

_____

_____

I *Observed*

I *Learned* _____

_____

_____

_____

_____

_____

I *Pray*

Devote yourselves to prayer, being watchful and thankful.
Colossians 4:2

Those in need of prayer

Thank you for answering my prayers _____

_____
_____
_____
_____
_____
_____
_____
_____
_____
_____

Lord we Praise your name

God gave us a spirit not of fear but of *power* and
love and self-control.
2 Timothy 1:7

WEEK *Seven*

I *will*

I'm *thankful* for _____

_____

_____

_____

_____

_____

_____

Verse to *live* by

Look to the LORD and his *strength*; seek his face always.
1 Chronicles 16:11

Those in need of *prayer*

Thank you for answering my prayers _____

_____
_____
_____
_____
_____
_____
_____
_____
_____
_____

Lord we *Praise* your name

Bible Journal

I *Thank* You for

I *Heard* You _____
_____
_____
_____
_____
_____

I *Observed*

I *Learned* _____
_____
_____
_____
_____
_____
_____

I *Pray*

Bible Journal

I Thank You for

I Heard You _____

_____
_____
_____
_____

I Observed

I Learned _____

_____
_____
_____
_____
_____

I Pray

Bible Journal

I Thank You for

I Heard You

_____

_____

_____

_____

_____

I Observed

I Learned

_____

_____

_____

_____

_____

_____

I Pray

Faith Journal

Dreams

Confessions

_____

_____
_____
_____
_____
_____
_____
_____
_____
_____
_____

God help me

Bible Journal

I Thank You for

I Heard You

_____
_____
_____
_____
_____

I Observed

I Learned

_____
_____
_____
_____
_____
_____
_____

I Pray

Bible Journal

VERSES READ   DATE

I *Thank* You for

I *Heard* You _____

_____

_____

_____

_____

I *Observed*

I *Learned* _____

_____

_____

_____

_____

_____

_____

I *Pray*

Bible Journal

I Thank You for

I Heard You

I Observed

I Learned

I Pray

Bible Journal

_____   _____

I Thank You for

I Heard You _____

_____

_____

_____

_____

I Observed

I Learned _____

_____

_____

_____

_____

_____

I Pray

You will pray to him, and he will hear you, and you will fulfill your vows.
Job 22:27

Those in need of prayer

Thank you for answering my prayers _____

_____

_____

_____

_____

_____

_____

_____

_____

_____

Lord we Praise your name

Let not your *hearts* be troubled, neither let them be
afraid.
John 14:27

WEEK *Eight*

I *will*

I'm *thankful* for _____

_____

_____

_____

_____

_____

_____

Verse to *live* by

You will seek me and find me, when you seek me with all your heart.
Jeremiah 29:13

Those in need of prayer

Thank you for answering my prayers _____

_____

_____

_____

_____

_____

_____

_____

_____

_____

_____

Lord we Praise your name

Bible Journal

VERSES READ   DATE

I *Thank* You for

I *Heard* You _____

_____

_____

_____

_____

I *Observed*

I *Learned* _____

_____

_____

_____

_____

_____

I *Pray*

Bible Journal

_____   _____
VERSES READ   DATE

I Thank You for

I Heard You _____

_____
_____
_____
_____

I Observed

I Learned _____

_____
_____
_____
_____
_____
_____

I Pray

Bible Journal

I Thank You for

I Heard You

_____

_____

_____

_____

_____

I Observed

I Learned

_____

_____

_____

_____

_____

_____

I Pray

Lord, do not hold this sin against them.
Acts 7:60

Dreams

Confessions

_____

_____
_____
_____
_____
_____
_____
_____
_____
_____
_____

God help me

Bible Journal

I *Thank* You for

I *Heard* You _____

_____

_____

_____

_____

I *Observed*

I *Learned* _____

_____

_____

_____

_____

_____

I *Pray*

Bible Journal

I Thank You for

I Heard You

I Observed

I Learned

I Pray

Bible Journal

I Thank You for

I Heard You

I Observed

I Learned

I Pray

Bible Journal

I Thank You for

I Heard You

_____

_____

_____

_____

_____

I Observed

I Learned

_____

_____

_____

_____

_____

_____

I Pray

Prayer Journal   You will pray to him, and he will hear you, and you will fulfill
your vows.
Job 22:27

Those in need of prayer

Thank you for answering my prayers _____

_____

_____

_____

_____

_____

_____

_____

_____

_____

_____

_____

Lord we Praise your name

Let not your *hearts* be troubled, neither let them be
afraid.
John 14:27

WEEK *Nine*

I *will*

I'm *thankful* for _____

_____

_____

_____

_____

_____

_____

Verse to *live* by

But I tell you, love your enemies and pray for those who persecute you.
Matthew 5:44

Those in need of prayer

Thank you for answering my prayers _____

_____

_____

_____

_____

_____

_____

_____

_____

_____

_____

Lord we Praise your name

Bible Journal

I *Thank* You for

I *Heard* You

I *Observed*

I *Learned*

I *Pray*

Bible Journal

I *Thank* You for

I *Heard* You

I *Observed*

I *Learned*

I *Pray*

Bible Journal

I Thank You for

I Heard You _____

_____

_____

_____

_____

I Observed

I Learned _____

_____

_____

_____

_____

_____

_____

I Pray

Faith Journal

Dreams

Confessions

_____

_____
_____
_____
_____
_____
_____
_____
_____
_____
_____
_____

God help me

Bible Journal

     DATE

I Thank You for

I Heard You

_____

_____

_____

_____

_____

I Observed

I Learned

_____

_____

_____

_____

_____

_____

_____

I Pray

Bible Journal

I Thank You for

I Heard You _____

_____
_____
_____
_____

I Observed

I Learned _____

_____
_____
_____
_____
_____
_____

I Pray

Bible Journal

VERSES READ   DATE

I Thank You for

I Heard You

_____

I Observed

I Learned

I Pray

Bible Journal

I *Thank* You for

I *Heard* You _____

_____

_____

_____

_____

I *Observed*

I *Learned* _____

_____

_____

_____

_____

_____

_____

I *Pray*

He will respond to the prayer of the destitute; he will not despise their plea.

Psalm 102:17

Those in need of prayer

Thank you for answering my prayers _____

_____

_____

_____

_____

_____

_____

_____

_____

_____

Lord we Praise your name

Trust in the Lord with all your *heart*, and do not
lean on your own understanding.
Proverbs 3:5-6

WEEK Ten

I will

I'm thankful for _____

_____
_____
_____
_____
_____
_____

Verse to live by

I call on you, my God, for you will answer me; turn your ear to me
and hear my prayer.

Psalm 17:6

Those in need of prayer

Thank you for answering my prayers _____

_____
_____
_____
_____
_____
_____
_____
_____
_____
_____

Lord we Praise your name

Bible Journal

I *Thank* You for

I *Heard* You _____
_____
_____
_____
_____
_____

I *Observed*

I *Learned* _____
_____
_____
_____
_____
_____
_____

I *Pray*

Bible Journal

_____   _____
VERSES READ   DATE

I Thank You for

I Heard You _____

_____

_____

_____

_____

I Observed

I Learned _____

_____

_____

_____

_____

_____

_____

I Pray

Bible Journal

I *Thank* You for

I *Heard* You _____

_____

_____

_____

_____

I *Observed*

I *Learned* _____

_____

_____

_____

_____

_____

I *Pray*

Lord, if You are willing, You can make me *clean*.

Matthew 8:2

Dreams

Confessions

God *help* me

Bible Journal

I *Thank* You for

I *Heard* You _____

_____
_____
_____
_____

I *Observed*

I *Learned* _____

_____
_____
_____
_____
_____

I *Pray*

Bible Journal

VERSES READ

DATE

I Thank You for

I Heard You _____

_____

_____

_____

_____

I Observed

I Learned _____

_____

_____

_____

_____

_____

_____

I Pray

Bible Journal

VERSES READ   DATE

I Thank You for

I Heard You

I Observed

I Learned

I Pray

Bible Journal

I *Thank* You for

I *Heard* You _____

_____
_____
_____
_____

I *Observed*

I *Learned* _____

_____
_____
_____
_____
_____

I *Pray*

Be joyful in hope, patient in affliction, faithful in prayer.

Romans 12:12

Those in need of prayer

Thank you for answering my prayers _____

_____

_____

_____

_____

_____

_____

_____

_____

_____

_____

Lord we Praise your name

Be strong, and let your heart take *courage*, all you
who wait for the Lord!
Psalm 31:24

WEEK *Eleven*

I *will*

I'm *thankful* for _____

_____

_____

_____

_____

_____

Verse to *live* by

And if we know that he *hears* us—whatever we ask—we know that we have what we asked of him.
1 John 5:15

Those in need of *prayer*

Thank you for answering my prayers _____

_____

_____

_____

_____

_____

_____

_____

_____

_____

_____

Lord we *Praise* your name

Bible Journal

I Thank You for

I Heard You

I Observed

I Learned

I Pray

Bible Journal

DATE

I Thank You for

I Heard You
_____

_____
_____
_____
_____

I Observed

I Learned
_____

_____
_____
_____
_____
_____
_____

I Pray

Bible Journal

I Thank You for

I Heard You

I Observed

I Learned

I Pray

Faith Journal

Dreams

Confessions _____

_____
_____
_____
_____
_____
_____
_____
_____
_____
_____
_____

God *help* me

Bible Journal

I *Thank* You for

I *Heard* You _____

_____

_____

_____

_____

I *Observed*

I *Learned* _____

_____

_____

_____

_____

_____

I *Pray*

Bible Journal

I *Thank* You for

I *Heard* You _____

_____

_____

_____

_____

I *Observed*

I *Learned* _____

_____

_____

_____

_____

_____

_____

I *Pray*

Bible Journal

I Thank You for

I Heard You _____

_____

_____

_____

_____

I Observed

I Learned _____

_____

_____

_____

_____

_____

I Pray

Bible Journal

I Thank You for

I Heard You _____

_____

_____

_____

_____

I Observed

I Learned _____

_____

_____

_____

_____

_____

I Pray

Devote yourselves to *prayer*, being watchful and thankful.
Colossians 4:2

Those in need of *prayer*

Thank you for answering my prayers _____

_____

_____

_____

_____

_____

_____

_____

_____

_____

_____

Lord we *Praise* your name

God gave us a spirit not of fear but of *power* and love and self-control.
2 Timothy 1:7

WEEK *Twelve*

I *will*

I'm *thankful* for _____

_____

_____

_____

_____

_____

_____

Verse to *live* by

Look to the LORD and his strength; seek his face always.
1 Chronicles 16:11

Those in need of prayer

Thank you for answering my prayers _____

_____
_____
_____
_____
_____
_____
_____
_____
_____
_____

Lord we Praise your name

Bible Journal

I *Thank* You for

I *Heard* You

I *Observed*

I *Learned*

I *Pray*

Bible Journal

_____
VERSES READ

_____
DATE

I *Thank* You for

I *Heard* You _____
_____
_____
_____
_____

I *Observed*

I *Learned* _____
_____
_____
_____
_____
_____
_____

I *Pray*

Bible Journal

I Thank You for

I Heard You _____

_____

_____

_____

_____

I Observed

I Learned _____

_____

_____

_____

_____

_____

I Pray

Lord, do not hold this sin against them.
Acts 7:60

Dreams

Confessions

_____

_____
_____
_____
_____
_____
_____
_____
_____
_____
_____

God help me

Bible Journal

I *Thank* You for

I *Heard* You

_____

_____
_____
_____
_____

I *Observed*

I *Learned*

_____

_____
_____
_____
_____
_____
_____

I *Pray*

Bible Journal

I Thank You for

I Heard You _____

_____

_____

_____

_____

I Observed

I Learned _____

_____

_____

_____

_____

_____

_____

I Pray

Bible Journal

I Thank You for

I Heard You _____

_____

_____

_____

_____

I Observed

I Learned _____

_____

_____

_____

_____

_____

I Pray

Bible Journal

I *Thank* You for

I *Heard* You _____
_____
_____
_____
_____

I *Observed*

I *Learned* _____
_____
_____
_____
_____
_____

I *Pray*

You will pray to him, and he will hear you, and you will fulfill your vows.
Job 22:27

Those in need of prayer

Thank you for answering my prayers _____

_____
_____
_____
_____
_____
_____
_____
_____
_____
_____

Lord we Praise your name

Let not your *hearts* be troubled, neither let them be
afraid.
John 14:27

_____

_____

_____

_____

_____

_____

_____

_____

_____

_____

_____

_____

_____

_____

_____

_____

_____

_____

_____

_____

_____

_____

_____

_____

_____

_____

_____

_____

_____

_____

_____

_____

WEEK *Thirteen*

I *will*

I'm *thankful* for _____

_____

_____

_____

_____

_____

_____

Verse to *live* by

Prayer Journal   You will *seek* me and find me, when you seek me with all your heart.
Jeremiah 29:13

Those in need of *prayer*

Thank you for answering my prayers   _____

_____

_____

_____

_____

_____

_____

_____

_____

_____

_____

Lord we *Praise* your name

Bible Journal

I Thank You for

I Heard You _____

_____
_____
_____
_____

I Observed

I Learned _____

_____
_____
_____
_____
_____
_____

I Pray

Bible Journal

_____

VERSES READ

_____

DATE

I Thank You for

I Heard You _____

_____

_____

_____

_____

I Observed

I Learned _____

_____

_____

_____

_____

_____

I Pray

Bible Journal

VERSES READ _____ DATE _____

I Thank You for

I Heard You _____

_____

_____

_____

_____

I Observed

I Learned _____

_____

_____

_____

_____

_____

I Pray

Lord, do not hold this sin against them.
Acts 7:60

Dreams

Confessions

_____

_____
_____
_____
_____
_____
_____
_____
_____
_____
_____
_____

God help me

Bible Journal

I Thank You for

I Heard You

_____
_____
_____
_____
_____

I Observed

I Learned

_____
_____
_____
_____
_____
_____

I Pray

Bible Journal

I Thank You for

I Heard You _____

_____

_____

_____

_____

I Observed

I Learned _____

_____

_____

_____

_____

_____

_____

I Pray

Bible Journal

VERSES READ

DATE

I Thank You for

I Heard You _____

_____

_____

_____

_____

I Observed

I Learned _____

_____

_____

_____

_____

_____

I Pray

Bible Journal

I *Thank* You for

I *Heard* You _____

_____

_____

_____

_____

I *Observed*

I *Learned* _____

_____

_____

_____

_____

_____

_____

I *Pray*

You will pray to him, and he will hear you, and you will fulfill your vows.
Job 22:27

Those in need of prayer

Thank you for answering my prayers _____

_____

_____

_____

_____

_____

_____

_____

_____

_____

_____

Lord we Praise your name

Let not your *hearts* be troubled, neither let them be
afraid.
John 14:27

_____

_____

_____

_____

_____

_____

_____

_____

_____

_____

_____

_____

_____

_____

_____

_____

_____

_____

_____

_____

_____

_____

_____

_____

_____

_____

_____

_____

_____

_____

_____

_____

_____

WEEK *Fourteen*

I *will*

I'm *thankful* for _____

_____

_____

_____

_____

_____

Verse to *live* by

But I tell you, love your enemies and pray for those who persecute you.
Matthew 5:44

Those in need of prayer

Thank you for answering my prayers _____

_____

_____

_____

_____

_____

_____

_____

_____

_____

Lord we Praise your name

Bible Journal

VERSES READ   DATE

I *Thank* You for

I *Heard* You

I *Observed*

I *Learned*

I *Pray*

Bible Journal

I Thank You for

I Heard You _____

_____

_____

_____

_____

I Observed

I Learned _____

_____

_____

_____

_____

_____

_____

I Pray

Bible Journal

I Thank You for

I Heard You

_____
_____
_____
_____
_____

I Observed

I Learned

_____
_____
_____
_____
_____
_____

I Pray

Faith Journal

For we live by faith, not by sight.
2 Corinthians 5:7

Dreams

Confessions

_____

_____

_____

_____

_____

_____

_____

_____

_____

_____

_____

God help me

Bible Journal

I Thank You for

I Heard You

I Observed

I Learned

I Pray

Bible Journal

I Thank You for

I Heard You

I Observed

I Learned

I Pray

Bible Journal

I Thank You for

I Heard You

I Observed

I Learned

I Pray

Bible Journal

I Thank You for

I Heard You

_____

_____

_____

_____

I Observed

I Learned

_____

_____

_____

_____

_____

I Pray

He will respond to the prayer of the destitute; he will not despise their plea.

Psalm 102:17

Those in need of prayer

Thank you for answering my prayers _____

_____

_____

_____

_____

_____

_____

_____

_____

_____

_____

Lord we Praise your name

Trust in the Lord with all your *heart*, and do not
lean on your own understanding.
Proverbs 3:5-6

WEEK *Fifteen*

I *will*

I'm *thankful* for _____

_____

_____

_____

_____

_____

_____

Verse to *live* by

I call on you, my God, for you will answer me; turn your ear to me and hear my prayer.

Psalm 17:6

Those in need of prayer

Thank you for answering my prayers _____

_____

_____

_____

_____

_____

_____

_____

_____

_____

_____

Lord we Praise your name

Bible Journal

I Thank You for

I Heard You

_____

_____

_____

_____

_____

I Observed

I Learned

_____

_____

_____

_____

_____

_____

I Pray

Bible Journal

I *Thank* You for

I *Heard* You

I *Observed*

I *Learned*

I *Pray*

Bible Journal

_____   _____

VERSES READ   DATE

I Thank You for

I Heard You _____

_____

_____

_____

_____

I Observed

I Learned _____

_____

_____

_____

_____

_____

I Pray

Lord, if You are willing, You can make me *clean*.

Matthew 8:2

Dreams

Confessions _____

_____
_____
_____
_____
_____
_____
_____
_____
_____
_____
_____

God *help* me

Bible Journal

_____   _____
VERSES READ   DATE

I *Thank* You for

I *Heard* You _____

_____

_____

_____

_____

I *Observed*

I *Learned* _____

_____

_____

_____

_____

_____

_____

I *Pray*

Bible Journal

VERSES READ _____ DATE _____

I Thank You for

I Heard You _____

I Observed

I Learned _____

I Pray

Bible Journal

I Thank You for

I Heard You

I Observed

I Learned

I Pray

Bible Journal

I Thank You for

I Heard You

I Observed

I Learned

I Pray

Be joyful in hope, patient in affliction, faithful in prayer.
Romans 12:12

Those in need of *prayer*

Thank you for answering my prayers _____

_____

_____

_____

_____

_____

_____

_____

_____

_____

Lord we *Praise* your name

Be strong, and let your heart take *courage*, all you
who wait for the Lord!
Psalm 31:24

WEEK *Sixteen*

I *will*

I'm *thankful* for _____

_____

_____

_____

_____

_____

_____

Verse to *live* by

And if we know that he hears us—whatever we ask—we know
that we have what we asked of him.
1 John 5:15

Those in need of prayer

Thank you for answering my prayers _____

_____
_____
_____
_____
_____
_____
_____
_____
_____
_____

Lord we Praise your name

Bible Journal

_____

VERSES READ

_____

DATE

I *Thank* You for

I *Heard* You _____

_____

_____

_____

_____

I *Observed*

I *Learned* _____

_____

_____

_____

_____

_____

_____

I *Pray*

Bible Journal

I *Thank* You for

I *Heard* You

I *Observed*

I *Learned*

I *Pray*

Bible Journal

I Thank You for

I Heard You

I Observed

I Learned

I Pray

Faith Journal

Dreams

Confessions _____

_____

_____

_____

_____

_____

_____

_____

_____

_____

_____

God *help* me

Bible Journal

I Thank You for

I Heard You

I Observed

I Learned

I Pray

Bible Journal

I Thank You for

I Heard You

I Observed

I Learned

I Pray

Bible Journal

I Thank You for

I Heard You

I Observed

I Learned

I Pray

Bible Journal

I Thank You for

I Heard You

I Observed

I Learned

I Pray

Devote yourselves to *prayer*, being watchful and thankful.
Colossians 4:2

Those in need of *prayer*

Thank you for answering my prayers _____

_____

_____

_____

_____

_____

_____

_____

_____

_____

_____

Lord we *Praise* your name

God gave us a spirit not of fear but of *power* and
love and self-control.
2 Timothy 1:7

WEEK *Seventeen*

I *will*

I'm *thankful* for _____

_____

_____

_____

_____

_____

_____

Verse to *live* by

Look to the LORD and his strength; seek his face always.
1 Chronicles 16:11

Those in need of prayer

Thank you for answering my prayers _____

_____

_____

_____

_____

_____

_____

_____

_____

_____

_____

Lord we Praise your name

Bible Journal

<u>VERSES READ</u>   <u>DATE</u>

I *Thank* You for

I *Heard* You _____
_____
_____
_____
_____

I *Observed*

I *Learned* _____
_____
_____
_____
_____
_____

I *Pray*

Bible Journal

I *Thank* You for

I *Heard* You

I *Observed*

I *Learned*

I *Pray*

Bible Journal

I Thank You for

I Heard You _____

_____

_____

_____

_____

I Observed

I Learned _____

_____

_____

_____

_____

_____

I Pray

Lord, do not hold this sin against them.
Acts 7:60

Dreams

Confessions

_____

_____
_____
_____
_____
_____
_____
_____
_____
_____
_____
_____

God help me

Bible Journal

I Thank You for

I Heard You

I Observed

I Learned

I Pray

Bible Journal

I Thank You for

I Heard You

_____

_____

_____

_____

_____

I Observed

I Learned

_____

_____

_____

_____

_____

_____

I Pray

Bible Journal

I Thank You for

I Heard You _____

_____

_____

_____

_____

I Observed

I Learned _____

_____

_____

_____

_____

_____

_____

I Pray

Bible Journal

_____   _____
VERSES READ   DATE

I _Thank_ You for

I _Heard_ You _____

_____

_____

_____

_____

I _Observed_

I _Learned_ _____

_____

_____

_____

_____

_____

I _Pray_

You will pray to him, and he will hear you, and you will fulfill
your vows.
Job 22:27

Those in need of prayer

Thank you for answering my prayers _____

_____

_____

_____

_____

_____

_____

_____

_____

_____

_____

Lord we Praise your name

Let not your *hearts* be troubled, neither let them be
afraid.
John 14:27

WEEK *Eighteen*

I *will*

I'm *thankful* for _____

_____

_____

_____

_____

_____

_____

Verse to *live* by

You will seek me and find me, when you seek me with all your heart.
Jeremiah 29:13

Those in need of prayer

Thank you for answering my prayers _____

_____

_____

_____

_____

_____

_____

_____

_____

_____

_____

Lord we Praise your name

Bible Journal

I Thank You for

I Heard You

I Observed

I Learned

I Pray

Bible Journal

I *Thank* You for

I *Heard* You _____

_____

_____

_____

_____

I *Observed*

I *Learned* _____

_____

_____

_____

_____

_____

_____

I *Pray*

Bible Journal

I Thank You for

I Heard You _____

_____

_____

_____

_____

I Observed

I Learned _____

_____

_____

_____

_____

_____

_____

I Pray

Faith Journal

Dreams

Confessions

_____

_____
_____
_____
_____
_____
_____
_____
_____
_____
_____
_____

God help me

Bible Journal

I Thank You for

I Heard You

I Observed

I Learned

I Pray

Bible Journal

I Thank You for

I Heard You _____

_____

_____

_____

_____

I Observed

I Learned _____

_____

_____

_____

_____

_____

_____

I Pray

Bible Journal

VERSES READ   DATE

I *Thank* You for

I *Heard* You _____
_____
_____
_____
_____

I *Observed*

I *Learned* _____
_____
_____
_____
_____
_____

I *Pray*

Bible Journal

I Thank You for

I Heard You

I Observed

I Learned

I Pray

You will *pray* to him, and he will hear you, and you will fulfill your vows.
Job 22:27

Those in need of *prayer*

Thank you for answering my prayers _____

_____

_____

_____

_____

_____

_____

_____

_____

_____

_____

Lord we *Praise* your name

Let not your *hearts* be troubled, neither let them be afraid.
John 14:27

SAMPLE *Journal*

I *will* not give in to the temptation to be normal. I will not allow my past to determine my future. I will stand firm in my belief that I have a God given purpose. It's my time to step up and allow God to work through me.

I'm *thankful* for giving me the vision and ability to achieve great things. Thank you for the power of prayer.

_____

_____

_____

_____

_____

Verse to *live* by You will seek me and find me, when you seek me with all your heart. Jeremiah 29:13

I Thank You for Giving your only Son so that I may live.

I Heard You   And if your eye causes you to stumble, gouge it out and throw it away. It is better for you to enter life with one eye than to have two eyes and be thrown into the fire of hell. Matthew 18:9

I Observed Jesus foresee his death and the betrayal by his disciples. All the disciples swear they would never betray Jesus. Jesus teaches the disciples that it is better to give up a part of your physical body than to risk not entering heaven.

I Learned Jesus was courageous. He was a man of his word. I am honored to be his child. Living by the word and understanding the word is so important. You must be courageous in your belief of the word. Never allow the idea of earthy possession to keep you from heaven.

I Pray That you enable me to learn the lessons of your Son. May your words guide me through this life. In Jesus name we pray, Amen.

I call on you, my God, for you will *answer* me; turn your ear to me and hear my prayer.

Psalm 17:6

Those in need of *prayer* Grandma Rose is sick and growing weak. The world seems to be going mad, pray for a positive change. People of God's Kingdom gain influence and use their passion, good, and faith to help change this world.

Thank you for answering my prayers   Thank you for cleansing my body of that awful bacteria and enabling me the strengthen to get back to work on my book

Lord we *Praise* your name   Bringing the idea of being an author idea into reality. Can't believe my books will be in people hands soon. I definitely didn't think my first book would be on this. I stayed open and you made it happen.

Lord, if You are willing, You can make me clean.

Matthew 8:2

Dreams I heard you loud and clear when you told me that it wasn't my turn yet. That I need not tell my story right now. I'm about 2 weeks from launching pre-sales. And I am putting one book down to create another. But I'm calm even though I'm changing my plan with no notice. I know this must be you guiding my steps. Because I typically don't do well without a plan.

Confessions I let my nerves get the best of me. I can't afford to be comfortable. But sometimes I let self doubt get in my way. I know that even if I doubt myself I must remember I have your.

God *help* me   Lord help me be bold. Don't allow me to hide the gifts you have given me. The world needs what I have. The world needs all the gifts you have stowed upon us. I pray I empower a generation to be bold and share their gifts.

ABOUT THE AUTHOR

ChellBee is a daughter of Christ, wife, and obsessive planner. Her passion for writing drove her to create a blog where she empowers women to embrace there imperfect journey. But along the way, she realized she would be doing a disservice if she failed to share how importance my faith has been throughout my journey. Creating and maintaining a lasting relationship with God is not always easy but with commitment, consistency, and the right tools its possible. She wanted to help women like her with all the above.

ChellBee grew up in the inner city of Compton, California, with her two sisters and mother. When she was 12, her family uprooted to the suburbs of Atlanta, GA where she later attended college. From a young age, she enjoyed writing in many different forms, from poetry and songs, to short story telling. Throughout her life writing allowed her to overcome the many personal obstacles she have faced.

Find more of ChellBee

Facebook: ChellBee
Instagram: @iamChellBee
Twitter: @iamChellBee
www.ChellBee.com

Made in the USA
Monee, IL
01 March 2022

92110199R00144